*Robin —*

# HOW TO
# WRITE A
# PROFESSIONAL
# BIO

*Here's to the future!*
*It's bright!*

**MCM**
**PUBLISHING**

MCM Publishing
2801 B Street, Ste. 111
San Diego, CA 92102

MCMPublishing.com

Copyright © 2020 Jeniffer Thompson

Book Cover and Interior Design by Monkey C Media
Edited by Lilli Kendle
Copyedited by All My Best
Author Photo by Chad Thompson Photography

Special Thanks to Marni Freedman, Tracy J. Jones, Aleta Reese and Melinda Martin

First Edition
Printed in the United States of America

ISBN: 978-0-9888882-9-6 (trade paperback), 978-0-9798551-8-4 (epub)

Library of Congress Control Number: 2019953115

JENIFFER THOMPSON

# HOW TO WRITE A PROFESSIONAL BIO

FOR AUTHORS

SPEAKERS &

ENTREPRENEURS

If you've ever dreaded
writing a bio, this one's for you.
You've got this!

# CONTENTS

**INTRODUCTION**     1

**PART ONE**

Step 1
Get Real with Your Goals     11

Step 2
Find Your Superpower     15

Step 3
Know Your Audience     25

Step 4
Identify Your Influencers     31

Step 5
Expand Your Bio Building Blocks     35

**PART TWO**

Step 6
Find Your Gold     45

Step 7
Follow Jeniffer's Smart Author Bio Formula     49

Step 8
Create Your Shitty First Draft     51

Step 9
Spin Your Story     61

Step 10
Connect the Dots     67

**PART THREE**

Case Study I: Rebecca Swift     81

Case Study II: Melissa Wright     87

Stellar Bio Examples     91

**ABOUT JENIFFER THOMPSON**     101

**LINKS AND RESOURCES**     103

# INTRODUCTION

Does your bio sparkle, and shine, and shout the best of you to the world? It better. A well-written bio is a critical piece of your author brand. And your bio is often your first introduction to the people who matter most—your audience.

If you're struggling to write a bio you're proud of, or unclear on how to even begin, then read on 'cause I wrote this book for YOU.

I'm going to walk you through this bio-writing business, one step at a time.

## Why Is Writing a Bio So Hard?

Okay, yes, I know, you've been taught to be humble, to avoid boasting, to wait for compliments to come to you. But your bio needs to include all of your goodness—it must. I want you to think of your bio as your fabulous introduction, the lights go down, the spotlight races toward you as you enter stage left, and the crowd goes wild.

Even if we separate the emotional side, writing a bio is hard. That compact little piece of copy needs to accomplish many things at once, and in as few words as possible.

In order to write a good bio, it's important to understand what a bio *is not*. Your bio is not a cover letter for a résumé, it isn't a CV (curriculum vitae), it isn't a boring account of what you've been up to for the past decade, nor is it a laundry list of accomplishments—i isn't a list of anything actually. It's a story. It's YOUR story.

A professional bio is your chance to control the narrative o YOU. It's your introduction into the world of the people who nee you most (that's right, I'm talking about your audience). Your bi is your pitch! And finally, here's something to think about: You're pitching your services because your audience needs you. We are going to make it about them.

You want a bio that

- ★ brags about you without coming off as a self-important ass,

- ★ fully represents who you are, but is really about your audience,

- ★ reveals a polished and professional presence,

- ★ establishes trust and credibility,

- ★ creates engagement by speaking to the needs of your audience, and

- ★ attracts the people who matter most—that audience I keep talking about (your future fans).

No wonder authors feel overwhelmed by the process. But fear not: I will guide you through ten easy steps to write and polish a stellar bio—a bio you'll be proud of.

## My First Bio

When I was fourteen, my English teacher directed me to write about myself without using the word "I." I still remember the feeling of my brain being squeezed and the knot in my belly that made me consider becoming a math major.

I'll never forget that exercise. Why? Because it worked. Without the "I" crutch, I had to think outside the box and imagine myself in a new way. That's exactly what I want you to do.

Imagine meeting yourself for the first time. What makes you unique? What about you is trustworthy? What have you done that is noteworthy? I want you to talk about yourself in the third person. Pretend like you're introducing a friend—an amazing, badass friend.

Once you've gotten the best of you onto paper, putting the pieces together is simply a matter of following my Smart Author Branding Bio Formula (don't worry, I'll guide you).

## What You Can Expect From This Book

We're not going to do this in one go. Ideally, I'd like you to break this into a two-week process where we cover Part One in the first week and Part Two in the second week. Of course, this is up to you. If you're in a hurry and just need to get this done, and get it done now, by all means—skip to Step 6 and start writing your bio now. But be sure to plan a time to revisit it so you can revise, polish, and make your bio the best it can be.

Part One of this book is all about the process of creating your bio building blocks. With each step, I'll ask you to answer a series of essential questions that will help you gather those building blocks. They are all about you, and the discovery of where you're going, and how you're going to get there. Your building blocks will become the foundation for a stellar bio that sings your praises and attracts your audience without sounding pompous. Yep, I'm going to help you write a bio you're proud of.

Part Two begins with my Smart Author Branding Bio Formula and a plan to put it all together. You'll learn how to present your credibility, prioritize your content, engage your audience, and incorporate a critical call to action—when you tell your audience what you want them to do, you create engagement and loyalty. I'll show you how to write several versions of your bio that each meet a specific need. I'll tell you how long each one should be and from what perspective to write them.

Plus, throughout this book, I'll include my Smart Author Branding tips to help you build your brand, your audience, and your visibility. After all, what's the point of an amazing bio if no one is reading it?

Finally, I share before-and-after examples[1] of bios that illustrate just how powerful a few simple word changes can be.

Still not convinced? Stay with me, you're going to rock at this. I promise.

## But Wait!
## What Is Smart Author Branding?

Smart Author Branding is about making smart choices, connecting the dots of your success, and believing that you are worthy of that success.

That last part is important. Are you worthy? As a branding expert, I have the honor of working with thought leaders and experts who have established themselves in their fields. They have honed in on their greatness and they offer a stellar service, but many of them lack one thing: *courage.* That is, the courage to believe in their value and to know they are worthy of a personal brand!

That's where I come in. I ask my clients to see themselves through a new lens. I help them identify their unique value and strengths and tap into the courage they need to take their business to the next level. If you are like my clients, you're a talented expert who has been educating yourself and honing in on your unique abilities for years, decades even. Seeing yourself through my lens asks you to recognize yourself as the expert you are. This is the secret to dominating in

---

1 Bio Case Studies in this book are from my past clients; I have changed the names and locations to protect their privacy.

your field and becoming a known thought leader. It takes courage to see yourself through that lens. It takes courage to believe in yourself.

You gotta have courage if you're gonna own it. And you gotta own it if you're going to be successful.

## It's Time to Access Your Courage

Here you are.
Stuck in the middle.
Looking for the courage to brag.

Courage is grace under pressure.

—*Ernest Hemingway*

## Be a Graceful Badass

You see, here's the thing. If you don't shout your expertise and badassery to the world, then the people who need you most will never find you. (Psst, I'm talking about your audience.)

It takes courage to step out of your comfort zone and disrupt the norm. It takes courage to shout your truth to the world and to *trust* that what you have to say is not only worthy but important, critical even.

As part of my Smart Author Branding series, I'm on a mission to help authors, speakers, and entrepreneurs access their courage. If you are ready to elevate your brand in a meaningful and lasting way, then your bio is the perfect place to start. And, like I said, I'll offer lots of tips along the way to keep up your momentum and shout your greatness loud and clear to the people who need your expertise now.

## My Promise to You

I'm going to hold your hand and guide you through a series of simple steps. Writing a bio isn't painful when you follow the steps, plug-in the data, and put one sentence in front of the other.

You cannot afford to put off the creation of your best bio any longer. *Today is the day.* As a thought leader, author, speaker, or entrepreneur, you will be asked for your bio over and over again. I can recall many occasions when out of the blue someone asked me to speak at a conference or contribute an article and they needed my bio (of a specific length) and they needed it *now.* Scrambling to get a bio off quickly will inevitably result in one that doesn't speak to its intended audience, or worse, is riddled with typos. Every subpar piece of content you send out will chink the armor of your personal brand.

This book is your first step in the Smart Author Branding process. Let's begin.

I think on some level, you do your best things when you're a little off-balance, a little scared. You've got to work from mystery, from wonder, from not knowing.

—Willem Dafoe

# PART ONE

*Step 1*

# GET REAL WITH YOUR GOALS

## What is Your End Goal?

What does success look like for you? Do you want to be a paid speaker? A published author? A known thought leader and disrupter? A media darling (you know, someone who gets invited onto CNN to talk about stuff they know a lot about)? Or maybe all of these things?

Whatever your success looks like, it's critical that you identify it now and get real with your goals—before you develop your brand, let alone write your bio. If you haven't identified your goals, you'll never be able to convey your purpose, and your audience won't get it either.

This may seem like a silly step, but sometimes being honest about what we want is the hardest part. "I want to be famous," or "I want to get paid what I'm worth," might feel like reaching into scary territory when you've been taught to be selfless, but if you can't own it right out of the gate, you'll never achieve it.

First things first: Know what you want your bio to accomplish. Next, what do you want people to do once they've read your bio?

If you're looking to be a paid speaker, then let people know you're a speaker right off. Let them know the benefits of hearing you speak. If speaking is your focus, own it; make it obvious. Your words guide people to an end: If you want people to buy your book, subscribe to your blog, or take your class, make it obvious and easy, provide links. There's no room for shyness when it comes to your bio—put it out there if you want good things to come back to you.

## Bio Building Blocks

★ What are your professional goals?

★ What does success look like for you?

★ Where do you want to be in three years? Five years? Ten years?

★ What do you want your bio to accomplish? You may have more than one answer, and that's okay, you'll have several versions of your bio. Each bio version will target a specific audience and have a unique set of goals.

★ What do you want people to do once they've read your bio?

_____

_____

_____

_____

_____

_____

_____

_____

_____

_____

_____

_____

_____

_____

_____

_____

_____

_____

_____

_____

_____

_____

_____

_____

_____

_____

_____

_____

_____

_____

_____

_____

_____

_____

_____

_____

_____

_____

_____

_____

_____

_____

_____

_____

*Step 2*

# FIND YOUR SUPERPOWER

## Who Are You?

Writing a bio feels like hard work because it requires you to be subjective about yourself—presumably the one thing you know more about than anything else. Of course you must be objective about the facts of your expertise, but, here's the deal: It's the "being subjective" part that makes your bio interesting.

Touting your worth is challenging for many people. This is especially difficult for women.

Ironically, we are attracted to confident people and people who know their value and own their worth. We expect our leaders to be confident and in control. Your bio needs to sing with confidence and exemplify your expertise and your strengths—you know, the things you are inherently good at, really good at. This is your superpower. There's no room for humility in your bio. The whole point is that you sound interesting, authoritative, and even impressive. Remember, you can write it in the third person, so you can brag without feeling like a braggart.

As a thought leader and an expert in your field, you already have the goods; you've put in your time and paid your dues. Now you just need to own it. It takes courage to tell your best story and allow yourself to boast a little.

I promise that the world will love you for it. Well, let's be clear, not everyone will love you. But we only need to reach the people who matter: your audience. In fact, if you're ruffling a few feathers, you're off to a great start—to appeal to the needs of everyone is to appeal to no one. That's where your voice and style come in. Allowing your personality to come through not only makes you interesting, it makes you memorable to the people who matter most.

## Your Strengths

I recommend that you purchase Strengths Finder 2.0 and take the online Gallup poll to discover your innate strengths. Author Tom Rath explains that strengths are actually talents, and only when we hone in on our talents and nurture them are we able to achieve success. His book is based on Don Clifton's StrengthsFinder system.

Knowing your strengths allows you to improve upon them and use them for good; like, for example, the good of your personal brand, and your unique story. Once you know what you are good at, you're able to more closely identify what makes you better than others in your field. Claiming the thing that makes you unique is the key to setting yourself apart from your competition, standing out, and being memorable.

## Authenticity

Writing your bio is the beginning of creating a successful personal brand complete with authority, far-reaching visibility, and authentic personal style. Did you just cringe a little when I used the word authentic? "Authentic" is one of those words that are so overused and maybe even a little cliché. Even so, it's a buzzword for a reason—people want more of it. With so many fake accounts, fake personas, and fake news, it's no wonder we as a culture are craving authenticity.

Being authentic is simple if you just "be," right?

It sounds ridiculous to say, "Yeah, I want my brand and bio to be authentic." Duh! But wait a minute. Let's think about this for a moment.... How often do you feel the need to put on a mask or show a certain side of yourself because the "real you" might offend some people? I say, go ahead and offend—the people you offend are clearly not your ideal clients.

Being authentic takes courage.

The truth is, when you go against the grain of who you are and what makes you happy, you cease being authentic. Letting your true self shine through in everything you do matters. It matters a lot.

Remember, you attract what you put out there. If you aren't being your authentic self, then you'll never be the person your audience needs you to be, which means you'll never attract the clients you truly identify with and who bring you joy. Besides, putting on an act is not sustainable.

## Voice

A key element of a personal brand is the voice in which you convey the story of you. Voice is the way you speak to your audience, and it's a critical part of brand development. Consider how the voice of your brand is received by your intended audience—how do you want people to perceive you?

What tone does your audience expect from you? If you're a discrimination attorney who caters mostly to academia, then an outrageous and unapologetic tone *might* be a poor choice. However, if you're an attorney who helps technology entrepreneurs and startups get off the ground, maybe an outrageous brand will help

you stand out from the crowd of seemingly endless options—the
are a lot of attorneys out there. Maybe slinging some lawyer shit-tal
is exactly what you need to get real and get noticed. Maybe? I kno
an attorney who did just that. And guess what? His firm is killing
with the twenty-something entrepreneurial crowd looking for a fir
that will help them reach their goals but that they can also relate t
and have fun with, not some stodgy old dudes who scowl a lot!

If you're happiest when you curse like a sailor and are you
outrageous self, then make sure your target audience will appreciat
your style. Do your research and know your audience and what the
expect, and then—deliver. And remember, just because everyone els
does it one way, that doesn't mean it's the right way. That firm
mentioned earlier? They are seriously pissing off the establishment
They are shaking it up. And that's a good thing, because they're
having a blast at lawyering and making a difference in their world. I
have a feeling they're going to be around a long time.

At the end of the day, your style and your voice must be true to
you, or it will never be sustainable.

Chances are, if you're not offending someone, you're probably
not doing it right. You cannot be everything to everyone. The more
some people love you and adore you, the more likely it is that others
will be turned off by you. Authenticity attracts loyal fans.

## What's Your Voice?

Is your voice authoritative? Casual? Blunt? Humorous? Maybe it's
serious or academic. Not sure? Remember, if it feels right, it probably
is. If you find yourself acting the part of someone whose personality
you shed on the weekends, you may be hiding your best self.

Are you naturally shy and reserved? Or, are you the life of
the party? Your voice may be a work in progress, and that's okay.
Branding is a journey—hopefully one where you're always striving
to be better. Success is never a straight line; it meanders and curves

and bends and even goes backward sometimes. Don't expect to get it right the first time. Instead, check in with your voice and the ways your audience responds to that voice, and then make the necessary corrections. A successful brand is always on a course of correction, and always evolving.

When you embrace your authentic voice and present your true self, your audience will find you!

Now, with that said, there's a time and place for everything. While the voice of your brand must be reflected in your bio, there may be occasion when you pull back on the casual or blunt tone and employ a more professional tone, like for your press kit, or your speaker bio. We'll get to industry standards and expectations for the various versions of your bio soon enough. But for now, I want you to identify your most authentic, comfortable, sustainable self.

## What Makes You So Special?

Let's imagine your experiences as a simmering sauce. Your whole life and all you've experienced are in that sauce, and it's been slowly building to exactly what you want it to be. Maybe there were some mistakes along the way—a little too much of something here, not enough of something there. But it's *your* special sauce, and you're learning how to make it just right. Your special sauce is directly related to your strengths.

As counterintuitive as it sounds, sometimes the best way to find your strength is to look at your weakness. My friend and writing coach, Marni Freedman, says that your gift is closest to your wound. Think about that. You are unique and special in your own way. The special sauce of *you* has been cooking and developing for a lifetime of learning, experience, hardship, and everything else that has shaped you into the person you are today.

A perfect example of this in action concerns one of my clients, Barbara. Barbara experienced an abusive childhood. And guess what?

Today she's an excellent child/family therapist because she employ empathy and she listens—she's been down in the trenches. Sh "gets it."

Whatever that "it" is for you—that's your superpower. That the thing that will make people want to read your book, pay t see you speak, take your class, and hire you. Failing to identif your superpower will leave you adrift and unmemorable in a se of competition.

Still not sure? Let's tackle this in a different way. Take a lool at the person who is already known in your industry—the persor who has more notoriety, more fame, and more success than you do What makes that person unique and special? How does she presen her superpower? Now, think about it further. Is there something you disagree with, or a way that she presents her message that you dislike? Mind you, I'm not promoting animosity or negativity—I want you to identify how you plan to do it better. What special causes do you have that she does not? What do you bring to the table that's different?

In brand positioning, we spend time identifying both your *point of parity* and your *point of difference*. Obviously you are going to be similar to your competition, but your competitive advantage will be the thing that makes you different.

If you open a record store across from the street from another record store, how do you get people to spend money in your store? Lower prices, a better selection, friendlier staff, or maybe a better return policy? Whatever it is, it's something that adds value to the customer experience. It's the thing that keeps them coming back.

Remember your special sauce? Maybe it's directly related to your passion. Let's say, for example, that you're a rock climber and you're looking for a better guidebook to a specific climbing area. All the guidebooks are confusing, and the topographic maps are unidentifiable. You nearly lost your ass on that last climb because you lost your route. So what do you do? You get fed up and decide to write a better book. Sometimes the thing that ruffles our feathers is the thing that makes us the most passionate about our topic.

What are you passionate about? I'll bet somewhere, buried within that passion, is your superpower!

## *Psst...*

Listen, I get it. This is not a simple process. I'm writing an entire book—yes, a full-length, get-down-deep-and-find-your-superpower book right now; this bio book is just a chapter in that larger book. And I can tell you right now that discovering your own personal strengths and talking about them is perhaps the toughest thing you'll ever do. But it will pay off in ways you never thought possible. A huge factor in success is believing in yourself and then having the courage to develop a brand that shouts it. This is *your story*! Okay, back to this bio writing business.

## Bio Building Blocks

For this set of building blocks, I recommend you enlist the help of your friends, colleagues, clients, and family to answer the questions. Sometimes what we can't see in ourselves is obvious to those closest to us. You might be surprised by what you discover.

★ What is your voice? (outrageous, funny, blunt, honest, dry, practical, reserved, critical, smart, etc.)

★ What type of content do you most enjoy communicating?

★ Do you feel you have to hold back for fear of offending people?

★ Do you come from an authentic place, or do you create a persona for yourself when you communicate?

★   What is your biggest strength?

★   What is your biggest weakness?

★   Why are people attracted to you?

★   Why do people work with you?

_____

_____

_____

_____

_____

_____

_____

_____

_____

_____

_____

_____

_____

_____

_____

_____

*Step 3*

# KNOW YOUR AUDIENCE

## Identify Your Target

First and foremost, who are you trying to attract? Who is your audience?

One of the most common answers I hear to this question is "everyone." And while it might be true that everyone *should* read your book, *everyone* is a tough target to hit. In fact, it's impossible. Narrowing your audience to a niche group will allow you to tap into the needs of that group in a granular and powerful way. Identifying your target is the only way to hit that target.

There are many ways to identify your audience, but let's start with you. Yes, *you*. You are, very likely, your ideal client. I mean, you wouldn't be so passionate about your topic if you weren't interested in it to begin with, right? When you started out, *you* were the audience. You still are. What did you expect and need from the experts? How did you find those experts? What social channels did you follow? What books did you read?

Identifying your competition allows you to see what and who your readers are engaging with. Follow those people on social, read their books, subscribe to their blogs, and listen to their podcast. Then see who follows those experts. Who is their audience?

Pay attention to the comments they leave. Find out what they're excited about and, conversely, what they complain about. What do they want more of? What else are they interested in? Next, go check out these people (the audience, that is) on their personal social channels. Get to know them. This is your audience too.

This will give you a clear lens into the language those other experts are using to reach your audience. What's working? What isn't working? Take a close look and not only will you identify your target, but you'll also discover what they want and need; and best yet, you'll begin to strategize a plan so you can do it better!

## Who's Paying Attention?

I encourage you to identify four or more comparable book titles in your field and then read the Amazon and GoodReads reviews for those books. Those reviewers, and the people who leave those comments, are your audience. They are the very people you need to reach, and everything you need to know about them is right there for the stalking. Yeah, stalking. You've just gotta dig in and pay attention. Then track everything you learn because it'll come in handy later.

## Point of View

Whether you write your bio in first person or third person has everything to do with your audience: who will be reading that bio and where will they be reading it.

For example, a website bio can be more casual—but should it be? It depends: Who's reading it, and what do they expect from you? If you're a self-help writer targeting teens, you may want to present your website bio in such a way that it speaks directly to those teens in the first person and tells them exactly how you can help them. On the other hand, if you are giving a commencement speech to the graduating class at Harvard, you're going to want a professional bio that introduces you in the third person. Remember, your bio is never really about you—it's about your audience.

In Step 9 I go into detail about all the possible versions of a bio you may need to write and the standards associated with each type of bio, including word count and point of view.

Still unsure? Read on. In the next step I'll talk about the value of knowing your influencers. You see, those influencers have already set the standard. You don't have to reinvent the wheel. You can see what is already resonating with your target audience and start there!

## Bio Building Blocks:

★ Identify four or more comparable titles.

★ Who is reviewing those books on Amazon and Goodreads? Pay Attention: What do they want and need?

★ Who will benefit most from your book?

★ Who needs your book right now?

★ Create a persona to identify your ideal client/fan/reader. As you make future decisions, always check in with that "person" to see if your bio and message resonates with him/her. No, it isn't a real person, that's true, but you can get surprisingly intimate with the needs of your audience when you think of him/her as a real, live person with needs, desires, fears, likes, and dislikes.

Be sure to check out my Links and Resources at the end of this book for a link to my free Persona Worksheet and other useful branding tools.

*Step 4*

# IDENTIFY YOUR INFLUENCERS

Knowing where you want to be gives you the ability to see who is there now. For example, if your goal is to land a traditional publishing deal, you'll want to identify authors who have recently done just that. Or, maybe you're a thought leader on women's leadership and want to be recognized on the TED stage, or you want to be known as a go-to expert in the media. You'd better know who's doing that now. These are the influencers in your industry. Pay close attention to what they're doing and how they're doing it.

Know this: Influencers are not necessarily competition—they are also the people who are hiring your competition, booking those speakers, reviewing those books, featuring guest bloggers to talk about your topic, or hosting a podcast. An influencer is anyone in the public eye who is currently influencing your target audience.

Stalk your influencers. Visit their websites, subscribe to their blogs and newsletters, follow them on social, and find out where they speak. Start a collection of their various bios: the short description they post on Twitter and Facebook, their longer LinkedIn version, the version they post on their website, the bio they include in their media/press kit, their book jacket bio, and their speaker bio. Notice what greatness they tout and what point of view they use to tell their story. Study them. Take what they do well, and consider how you can improve the message of your bio.

You'll find that all the versions of a person's bio will have one thing in common—voice. The essence of that person will remain true; it's the specifics and tone that may change from one version to the next. I'll talk more about this in Step 8, when you create the various versions of your bio.

Don't worry. You can do this. One step at a time.

## Bio Building Blocks:

★ List your top three to five influencers.

★ What are they doing that you agree with?

★ What are they doing that you disagree with?

★ How can you do it better?

★ What makes their bio shine?

★ Where does their bio fall flat?

_____

_____

_____

_____

_____

_____

_____

_____

_____

_____

_____

_____

_____

_____

_____

_____

_____

_____

_____

_____

_____

_____

_____

_____

_____

_____

_____

_____

_____

*Step 5*

# EXPAND YOUR BIO BUILDING BLOCKS

Congratulations! You've already created your building blocks for a stellar bio. You now know

★ Your Goals (what you want to accomplish),

★ Your Superpower (what makes you unique),

★ Your Audience (who you're targeting), and

★ Your Influencers (the people who already reach your target audience).

Keeping that in mind, it's time to lay it down. Just dig in and start writing.

Don't panic. Don't even think about it. This is not a test—seriously, just lay it all down.

Go wild. Say it all.

Be you. Include everything. Include clichés with abandon. Be funny. Be sarcastic. Be honest. Be YOU.

Still not ready? Okay, then, think of it this way: This first version of your bio is really more of an information dump. You'll pick out all the gold later. If it's easier for you to create a bulleted list, go right ahead; we'll make sense of it later.

Once you've completed your information dump, step back from your writing. Take a few days to let it sit and churn in your mind. Assign a notebook that you keep on hand to jot down more ideas and additional things to include. I guarantee your brain will be coming up with all sorts of things you're not going to think of now. Be sure to capture everything that comes to mind over the next several days. I'm a huge fan of documenting all of your aha moments and research results in a notebook. If you don't already have a system in place for capturing and organizing these thoughts, check out the link to my Getting Organized Tips sheet in the Links and Resources at the back of this book.

As you take time to sit with your bio and consider the parts that matter most, I'd like you to consider some words of wisdom I stole from my friend Marni Freedman: "Staring out the window counts." Sometimes the best thing we can do as writers is let our stories take shape in our brains and allow time for reflection. Many creatives need a certain amount of procrastination in order to let our best ideas fully develop and take shape.

Be gentle with yourself, but also give yourself a deadline to make it happen. A reasonable amount of staring-out-the-window time can be therapeutic, but too much is detrimental to your goal. Be gentle with yourself, but get it done.

## Bio Building Blocks

If you're not quite sure how to lay it all down, then begin by answering the following questions:

- ★ What do you do, exactly? Be literal.

- ★ What is your primary focus, the thing you are most passionate about?

★ What is your mission?

★ What is the number one thing you want people to know about you?

★ Why does your ideal client need your service or book?

★ How can you help your audience?

★ How do you do it differently from your competitors?

★ What are your competitors doing wrong?

★ Why did you decide to go into your line of work in the first place?

★ What are your educational credentials?

★ What experience do you have?

★ Have you been featured anywhere? In the news, published articles, podcasts, on blogs?

★ Have you ever presented your topic in person to an audience?

★ Have you written any books?

★ Why did you decide to write your book?

★ Do you have a podcast or blog?

★ Are you a consultant?

★ Who are your clients?

★ Do you belong to any associations?

★ Have you won any awards?

★ What do you want your audience to do after they finish reading your bio?

Now, write it.

Then, let it sit for a few days. Take some time to let this sink i
before you review it again. Be prepared to jot down anything tha
comes to mind during the next few days.

Remember, staring out the window counts.

_____

_____

_____

_____

_____

_____

_____

_____

_____

_____

_____

_____

_____

_____

_____

_____

_____

_____

_____

_____

_____

_____

_____

_____

_____

_____

_____

_____

_____

_____

_____

_____

_____

_____

_____

_____

_____

_____

_____

_____

_____

_____

_____

_____

_____

_____

_____

_____

_____

_____

_____

_____

_____

_____

_____

_____

_____

_____

_____

_____

_____

_____

_____

_____

_____

_____

_____

_____

_____

_____

_____

_____

_____

_____

_____

Believe you can and you're halfway there.

—Theodore Roosevelt

# PART TWO

*Step 6*

# FIND YOUR GOLD

We're about to get busy with your words and make some serious sense out of your value and authority. Ready?

Let's do this!

It's time to revisit your work with fresh eyes and highlight anything that jumps out as particularly relevant. You can literally print out your information dump and highlight, circle, or underline anything that sounds good. High-five if you don't want to waste paper, I admire your sense of environmental awareness—go ahead and highlight the text digitally. Do what works best for you, as long as you find your gold.

At this stage, as you highlight and identify the best of you, I'd like to get you thinking about the ingredients of a stellar bio. Here's a first look at my formula.

## Jeniffer's Smart Author Bio Formula

1. **Your Focus:** What do you do, exactly? Examples: Author, Researcher, Speaker, Serial Entrepreneur, Political Scientist, Branding Expert, Writing Coach, Chief Inspirational Coach, etc. This is the thing that people need to know right out of

the gate, the thing that sets the stage and gives your reader context.

2. **Your Grabber:** This is the thing that grabs your potential reader. How does your focus affect them? What makes you unique? Feel free to inflate and throw in some keywords like *passion, purpose*, and *vision*.

3. **Your Credibility:** What gives you the right to be an expert? What dues have you paid? Include education, awards, and experience. Know this: Experience is big-time important; you don't have to be a Harvard graduate to know what the hell you're doing. I never went to bio-writing school, and look at me, I'm writing a book on it. Why? Because I've written thousands of bios (and you can too).

4. **Your Promise:** How will you help your reader? What, specifically, do you offer your potential reader or client? Name it: a specific service or offer, your book, your blog, weekly podcast, a workshop or course you teach, etc. This will be something you are proud of that your audience will benefit from now. It's okay to name more than one, but keep it brief and on-point—the thing you are most excited about and that your reader will be excited about too. I like to think of this part as an information gap: you have information that your readers want. Make it clear what that is so they want more of you.

5. **Your More:** This is where you beef up your street cred—these are things that go beyond your education: associations you belong to, boards you serve on, places you teach, organizations where you have spoken, more books you have written, and places where you have been featured (like newspapers, magazines, TV Shows, podcasts, and other books that mention you). List a few reputable clients, but only if

your audience will recognize them. And finally, do you have any shining endorsements from influencers in your area of expertise? Clip a few words (and only a few words) and use them to tout your deliciousness. Something like this: *Time Magazine* says "she's the best thing since sliced avocados." (Seriously, avocados are delicious!)

6.  **Your CTA (call to action):** What do you want people to do: Visit your website? Follow you on social? Follow your blog, buy your book, or take your class? Tell your readers what you want them to do and how they can get more of you—or you've wasted your hard-earned money on this book, not to mention the time it's taken you to read it, and write a bio!

It's time to highlight all those words you dumped on the page in Step 5. It's time to get real with your bio-writing self. Look everything over—all your words—and consider the parts that fit into this formula. The best, most delicious ingredients of you; remember that simmering sauce? And if you're inspired to add more words, have at it. Just remember to highlight the parts that ring true. We'll plug them into my formula next, in Step 7.

Take your time with this. Remember, just keep the gold. These are the words that will make you stand out and shine.

*Step 7*

# FOLLOW JENIFFER'S SMART AUTHOR BIO FORMULA

Now that you've identified your key ingredients, it's time to plug 'em into the formula. This is the fun part. We're still not concerned about polishing, but if you're so inspired to wax poetic, by all means, go to it. For now, our goal is to get all the right parts in the right places. We'll fret over the details and polish your story soon enough. I include a link to a blank worksheet in my Links and Resources section as well.

1. Your Focus: _____

_____

_____

_____

2. Your Grabber: _____

_____

_____

_____

3. Your Credibility: _____

_____

_____

_____

4. Your Promise: _____

_____

_____

_____

5. Your More: _____

_____

_____

_____

6. Your CTA (call-to-action): _____

_____

_____

_____

*Step 8*

# CREATE YOUR SHITTY FIRST DRAFT

It's time to write your story.

Anne Lamott coined the term *shitty first draft* in 1995, but I first heard it from Marni Freedman—somehow it just makes you feel better and gives you permission to write without judgment! Marni does that: She's always giving writers permission to write, in fact, she wrote a book on it, *Permission to Roar: for Female Thought Leaders Ready to Write Their Book.* I include a link to her book and other powerful resources in the back of this book.

I want you to do that now. I want you to *roar.* No judgment, just write.

Begin by getting your bio to a place where it's pretty good, or even pretty shitty. It doesn't have to be great—not yet. The main thing is that you just get it written. Once you feel reasonably confident that you've got it all there, go ahead and run it by those who know you best, the ones who will be honest with you, who won't shoot you down or trip up your confidence. This is key. Destructive criticism kills our creative spirit. Protect yourself.

Be prepared to consider the advice that makes sense, and throw out what doesn't. Then focus on the shape of your story. It's all there, but does it have a clear message? Reach out to supporters, mentors, clients, fans, and colleagues to get their feedback.

## Remember Your Courage

This might be the time to dig down and grab hold of that courage we talked about. Let's get real.

- ★ Does your bio reflect your goals?

- ★ Does it reflect your superpower?

- ★ Does it include the best of you?

- ★ Did you hold back?

- ★ Is it honest?

- ★ Does it reflect your joy and your voice?

- ★ Does it speak directly to your audience and tell them why they need you?

- ★ Does it provide a call to action?

## How Long Should It Be?

Don't cut or stretch your story needlessly. The most important thing is that it speaks to your audience and represents you well. If you are worried about how many words your bio should be, I'd like to encourage you to forget about word count for now.

I want to be clear about something: Your bio needs to be the right length for YOU. I know, I get it, we humans like rules. Don't worry, I'll provide general word-count guidelines in Step 9. For now, just know that a professional bio can range anywhere from 80 to 800 words. It really depends on how much you have to say and convey.

Ultimately, your bio needs to be the best of you. If you're still not sure, take a look at the following example. Also, check out my bio case studies in the back of this book, where I dissect my formula and show that *how* you say something is just as important as *what* you say.

## Smart Author Bio Example:

Maria Rodriguez-Stamm is an entrepreneur, writer, and lifelong advocate for women. She is a dynamic speaker and facilitator, and most recently, the host of the BRAVA podcast. She is passionate about helping midlife women start and grow their own businesses as a path to personal and economic growth. Maria has a Bachelor's degree in Biology from the University of California, San Diego, and a PhD in epidemiology from the University of California, Davis. Her dissertation research focused on women's use of alternative medicine during menopause because she was fascinated by the concept of women aging on their own terms—much like her current stance on women in business.

After nearly three decades working in health care as an administrator, a researcher, and consultant, Maria founded BRAVA Women in 2017. Dissatisfied with business resources that seemed produced by and for people very unlike her, Maria decided to create a community and an array of products that speak to midlife women entrepreneurs who want to see and hear from others like themselves who are passionate about their work and their lives.

Maria is a graduate of the HOPE Latina Leadership Institute and has served on the California Women's Health Council and on numerous nonprofit boards. Maria's podcast can be found on iTunes or wherever you get your podcasts. To get your free **Bring Your Brave**™ vision map and join the BRAVA women's movement, visit Example.com.

Let's look at the parts and see how Maria plugged her story into the formula:

1. **Maria's Focus**: Maria Rodriguez-Stamm is an entrepreneur, writer, and lifelong advocate for women; she is a dynamic speaker and facilitator and, most recently, host of the BRAVA podcast.

2. **Maria's Grabber**: She is passionate about helping midlife women start and grow their own businesses as a path to personal and economic growth.

3. **Maria's Credibility**: Maria has a Bachelor's degree in Biology from the University of California, San Diego and a PhD in epidemiology from the University of California, Davis. Her dissertation research focused on women's use of alternative medicine during menopause because she was fascinated by the concept of women aging on their own terms—much like her current stance on women in business. After nearly three decades working in health care as an administrator, a researcher, and consultant, Maria founded BRAVA Women in 2017.

4. **Maria's Promise**: Dissatisfied with business resources that seemed produced by and for people very unlike her, Maria decided to create a community and an array of products that speak to midlife women entrepreneurs who want to see and hear from others like themselves who are passionate about their work and their lives.

5. **Maria's More**: Maria is a graduate of the HOPE Latina Leadership Institute and has served on the California Women's Health Council and on numerous nonprofit boards.

6. **Maria's CTA (call to action)**: Maria's podcast can be found on iTunes or wherever you get your podcasts. To get your free "Bring Your Brave"™ vision map and join the BRAVA women's movement, visit Example.com.

## The Power of Words

Words affect us on a deep level; they affect our perceptions, our emotions, and our beliefs. Words guide us to conclusions. By placing emphasis on a particular word, you can change the meaning of the overall message and draw in your audience.

You have the ability to evoke emotion, to tap into someone's desires or fears, and to influence your reader to take action—simply by the words you choose. Your most powerful and persuasive marketing tool will be your choice of words.

The power of persuasion is the secret sauce of successful marketing.

Your bio is your own personal marketing copy—we are packaging YOU and framing the perception of YOU for your target audience.

Here are a few tips to consider when choosing the most powerful words that will package YOU.

★ Be direct and clear; use simple and concise language.

★ Use discretion and pacing.

★ Include short sentences for impact.

★ Use active verbs to motivate and encourage action.

★ Use positive and optimistic language to instill hope.

Below is a list of positive words to consider when you want to instill trust in your reader:

| | | |
|---|---|---|
| ★ commitment | ★ prosperity | ★ prosperity |
| ★ strength | ★ courage | ★ protect |
| ★ success | ★ empower | ★ reform |
| ★ passion | ★ lead | ★ share |
| ★ moral | ★ hard work | ★ tough |
| ★ legacy | ★ movement | ★ truth |
| ★ opportunity | ★ principle | ★ vision |

Also consider the emotional impact of your words. For example, airlines don't have "life preservers," they have "flotation devices." One sounds scary and makes me feel panicky, the other one gives me confidence that I won't drown. If you use words that have a positive connotation, your readers or listeners will, by default, feel positive even if they don't consciously realize it.

## Styles of Writing

When it comes to writing copy, I recommend that you choose a style and stick with it. For most authors, *The Chicago Manual of Style* is recommended, because that is what the publishing industry uses and expects. Because I am a journalist, though, I learned AP Style and often use that in writing press releases and media bios. There are four styles of writing:

1. **Associated Press (AP)**: most commonly used by journalists.

2. **American Psychological Association (APA)**: commonly used in the social sciences.

3. **The Chicago Manual of Style**: arguably the most comprehensive; usually used in book publishing.

4. **Modern Language Association (MLA)**: the most common style among non-writers; typically used in a public school setting.

It's important that your copy is consistent. For example, if you spell out your numbers in one paragraph, and then use numerals in another, you'll appear unpolished and unprofessional. Consistent usage of the Oxford Comma (sometimes called a serial comma) is a common inconsistency among writers: AP style advises against using the Oxford comma, while Chicago always uses it. I personally care about and use the Oxford comma when I write for non-media purposes. But, know this dear bio-writing friend: I rely on my editor to make sure I never forget! (Thank you, editor).

Have a conversation with your copyeditor about what style you would like to follow so that he/she will help you stay on track. Seriously, you do not need to learn styles and become an editor—that's why we hire editors! Concentrate on your writing, not your editing skills.

## Your Shitty First Draft

_____

_____

_____

_____

_____

_____

_____

_____

_____

_____

_____

_____

_____

_____

_____

_____

_____

_____

_____

_____

_____

_____

_____

_____

_____

_____

_____

_____

_____

_____

_____

_____

_____

_____

_____

_____

_____

_____

_____

*Step 9*

# SPIN YOUR STORY

Review the formula. Did you remember all your juicy details? Is it all there? What's missing?

It's time to consider. Revise. Rinse. Repeat.

## Spin Your Truth

Okay, to be clear, I am not suggesting that you lie. Here's the deal: Sometimes being vague allows the reader to invest their own values and needs into their perception of YOU and what YOU offer. For example, do you have eight years of experience in your field? That's nearly a decade, and a decade sounds better than eight years. Are you offering "50 Percent Off" your seminar series, or do you have a "Buy One, Get One Free" deal? The word "Free" connotes a positive feeling of getting something for nothing, and who doesn't want that?

Write your story with energy, confidence, and conviction. Don't be afraid to use words like *empower*, *passion*, and *success*! You are not just presenting your story, you are persuading your audience that your story matters to them.

## Use Just the Good Stuff

Brevity is key when it comes to drawing people in, especially those who have never heard of you: Don't bore us, get to the chorus. With that said, take it slow. This is a process; whittling away at your bio should happen slowly and methodically. Psst: Saving every version of your whittling process will serve useful later when you're ready to embark on your personal branding journey. (It's all good messaging fodder.) Remember, this is the gold—you don't want any of it to slip through your fingers.

## Forget the Rules

Wait, what? That's right—you heard me. When it comes to writing your bio, these are only suggestions for getting started, mere guidelines to help you begin. There are no hard and fast rules for writing your bio. Write what feels right for you. Write one version, or write twenty. Don't sweat the small stuff. Switch it up. Write in the first person. Write in the third person. Forget the formula. Just begin. And then check in often. The key to success lies at the heart of your personal truth. Be authentic. Courageously tout. Consistently check in. Remain relevant to your audience. Be true to you. Have fun!

## And Ask for Help

Share your polished bio with other industry leaders and influencers you have a good relationship with. They might have insight into the needs of your audience and know what is expected within your industry. They might have professional recommendations you've overlooked.

## Your Polished Bio

_____

_____

_____

_____

_____

_____

_____

_____

_____

_____

_____

_____

_____

_____

_____

_____

_____

_____

_____

_____

_____

_____

_____

_____

_____

_____

_____

_____

_____

_____

_____

_____

_____

_____

_____

_____

_____

_____

*Step 10*

# CONNECT THE DOTS

It's time to build your arsenal of bio versions so that you're prepared for any situation that requires a bio. For most professionals, the standard is two versions: a long one and a short one. However, I'd like you to think beyond the typical. Be exceptional in every aspect of your brand.

You never know how someone will discover you. That's why the nuance of each bio you put out there is so important. This is your opportunity to establish a good first impression and engage your potential audience, to get them to want more—no matter the situation.

Every version of your bio will have a specific purpose. Preparing for all possibilities puts you in control of your story. Below I provide a list of possibilities to consider, from your casual to your professional, from LinkedIn to Twitter. It all counts.

## Here's a run-down of some possibilities:

1. **Website "About Me" Bio:** If you've heard me speak, or read my book, *Website WOW: Turn Your Website into Your Most Powerful Marketing Tool*, then you know your website is

your home base—the message you convey there controls th
narrative of YOU. On your About Me page, you have a
opportunity to have fun with it. Think of this as more of a
initial, in-person conversation with a potential client. You
personality and passion need to jump off the screen and spea
directly to that person.

Remember, your website is where people go to learn more
about YOU, to get to know YOU better, and to connect with
YOU on a deeper level. Readers expect to get a little extra.
It's totally okay to include details about your personal life,
hobbies, and, well, whatever you like. It's your bio; go wild
(if it makes sense for your brand goals, of course). Ultimately,
the tone you take on will depend on your personality, your
goals, and your audience expectations.

My academic clients keep their bios very professional and
write in the third person, while my fiction- and memoir-
author clients tend to write a first-person, casual bio that
makes readers feel like they are enjoying a casual conversation
over tea.

Your website bio is your all-in, extended-length version that
fully represents you, your expertise, and your personality.
Your website bio can be as long as you think it needs to be.
Plus, consider including little extras, little delicious morsels
that make your reader feel special, like a timeline of the
important milestones in your life, or "Ten Things You Don't
Know About Me."

★ Recommended length: 300 to 1,500 words. Whoa!
Really? Yep, you heard me. The truth is, it doesn't
really matter how many words it is, as long as it doesn't
bore your reader to tears, or lack anything useful.

★ Point of view: Depends on your intended audience. For a more professional feel, write this bio in third person. To connect with your audience on a more personal level, write it in first person.

2. **Book Jacket or Back Cover Bio**: In general, book jacket bios tend to be short and sweet and a little bit casual. Include details that make you noteworthy as the author of that particular book. Research what other authors in your genre are doing and start there. If you've written your book to establish your expertise, then definitely highlight your credibility and the thing you want to be known for. If you've written other noteworthy books that will help sell this book, include those as well. Most authors include a short sentence with personal information, like: *Joanne lives in San Diego with her husband and two ferocious pugs.* It's totally acceptable to be a little funny and show some personality, as long as that's true to your brand goals and your brand voice.

   ★ Recommended length: 25 to 95 words.

   ★ Point of view: Third person.

3. **Media Bio**: If you're looking for national media attention and to get called upon as an expert, you'll want a powerful media bio that follows the rules. Short, to the point, and packed with a punch. Focus on the elements of your expertise that will advance your goals. Remember, your bio tells people what you want them to know about you and how you can fill a specific need. Producers and journalists are looking for experts to provide value and real-life experience, as well as statistics and facts, to their story; they want to know that you have authority on a subject and that you are credible.

   A professional media bio will follow the Associated Press style of writing. For example, the first mention of your name will include your full name, while each subsequent reference will include your last name only. Second reference example: "Thompson is the leading expert on personal branding." An interviewer or producer is more likely to quote your bio word-for-word if it's in line with their style of writing, plus this shows further professionalism on your part. Psst: Hire a copyeditor to keep it clean.

★ Recommended length: 80 to 125 words.

★ Point of view: Third person.

4. **Speaker Bio:** A speaker bio will speak directly to the target audience of that particular speaking engagement. For that reason, you might need several versions of your speaker bio. Begin with a base formula; something similar to your media bio will work great.

Remember, your bio is your introduction to a group of people who may or may not have ever heard of you. Before submitting your bio, do your research, take a look at the bios of past speakers and ask for an attendee list (a past list will work too) to see how you can offer the most value. What is their primary objective? Your bio may be the thing that determines whether or not someone will attend your talk. Also, it's important to know that many conference programs require a limited number of characters or words. Know that limit and submit appropriately to avoid the need for a conference organizer to cut your bio for you—you need to control your bio, not someone else. If you are armed with several lengths that each highlight the best of you, you'll be prepared for anything.

★ Recommended length: 80 to 125 words.

★ Point of view: Third person.

5.  **Contributor Byline Bio**: These days most articles are published online and will include a short bio after the article, as well as your byline and a link to a longer, albeit still pretty short bio. *Forbes, Huffington Post,* and *Mashable* are examples. See what other writers are doing in your genre and follow their lead, but be sure to add your own style and flare.

    ★  Recommended length: around 120 words.

    ★  Point of view: Third person.

6.  **LinkedIn Bio**: There's no minimum word count, but people viewing you on LinkedIn are likely to be colleagues, conference organizers, and people who can move your career forward. So, again, who's your audience and what are your goals? I know, I'm beginning to sound like a broken record but, seriously, this is important. A balance between your speaker and casual bio is a good bet. Just enough personality to make you interesting and likable while also presenting a bio that sings your praises and drives the point home that you are credible, have authority, and are an important person to know.

    ★  Recommended length: 150 to 300 words.

    ★  Point of view: LinkedIn tends to have more of a professional audience and therefore people expect professionalism. For that reason, I recommend writing this bio in the third person. (If you're not sure, see what other influencers are doing currently.)

7.  **Facebook Bio**: At the time of this writing, there is an intro space to the right of your Facebook profile where you tell people, in 15 words or fewer, what you're all about. This is your personal headline and it needs to deliver a punch. When I was in college I took a class on headline writing. We had a

predefined amount of space in which to fit our headline—it had to engage the reader and tell them what the article was about in a specific number of characters, no more, no less. It was brutal. I loved it.

Headline writing is an art form. Spend some time on yours. Tell your reader who you are and why they should care. Plus, with Facebook, you will also post a longer version of your bio in your *About* section. Remember, "Don't bore us, get to the chorus." You've got to speak to your audience. Also makes sure it reflects both your goals and the goals of your reader. I personally feel that if you are on Facebook, then your audience expects a little more casual tone and it's okay to share a version of your casual bio in all its glory.

★ Recommended length: 15 words + 100 to 300 words.

★ Point of view: First person.

In addition to the preceding versions, you'll be posting super-short versions on your various social channels, as well as other online profiles to help build visibility for your brand. These are equally important and require attention. Below is a short list with recommendations to consider.

8. **Twitter**

★ 160 characters (about 20 words). Make it count.

★ Third person.

9. **Medium**

★ 160 characters (about 20 words). Make it count.

★ Third person.

10. **Instagram**

★ 150 characters. You know the drill. You've got this.

★ Third person.

11. **YouTube**

   ★ 154-word description. Brief and to the point. I recommend you add personality here.

   ★ First person.

12. **Amazon Author Central page**

   ★ No word limit. I recommend between 250 and 500 words. Be sure to include your website URL in the last line of your bio; it will not serve as a live link, but people will be able to easily find your website if you give them the URL.

   ★ Third person.

13. **Goodreads**

   ★ 2,000 characters; Goodreads allows for live links, so be sure to follow their formatting tips and insert an active link back to your website, as well as links to your books.

   ★ Third person.

14. **BookBub**

   ★ Recommended length: 150 to 350 words.

   ★ Third person.

# Taking Inventory

Which bio versions will you need? Are there other versions that are not listed here? Check out the following worksheet. Plus, I've included a link in the back of this book to download blank worksheets.

## Version _____ (fill in the blank)

Who'll be reading this bio?

_____

_____

Is there an expected standard for this version of your bio?

_____

What is the most important takeaway, the thing you want people reading this version to know about you first and foremost?

_____

_____

_____

Set a goal for this bio version. What does it need to accomplish? Is it meant to get clients? Convince people to attend your seminar? Read your book? Hire you? Or, position you?

_____

_____

_____

Create a call-to-action where you literally ask people to do something: subscribe to your blog, buy your book, take your class, download your tips sheet, contact you, etc.

_____

_____

_____

## The Final Touches

When your bio versions are complete, have them edited by a professional copyeditor.

Be sure to check in with, and update, your bio every three months. The last thing you need is a rusty bio. Schedule an alert on your calendar. As your goals change and your experience increases, it will be critical to keep your bio up to date. This is what I call "connecting the dots of your success."

Every step you take to polish your brand will pay off and allow you more time to do what you love. And remember, your fans want a reason to check in and stay connected to you. Updating your bio and headshot is just one of the ways to get attention, stay connected and, more importantly, stay relevant.

I've developed a spreadsheet to help you keep track of the online profiles you will create and the numerous places where you will submit your bio. This is a great way to remember where your story is getting visibility and ensure that your story remains relevant. Check out the Links and Resources in the back of this book for the link to this and other helpful worksheets.

As an author and entrepreneur, you've got to work smarter, not harder. Stay connected to your audience and, more importantly, stay connected to your own journey and your goals. Remember your joy—after all, you have an important message to share with the world! Your audience is out there, waiting for you. Go get 'em!

P.S. Oh, and also let me know how it goes! If you are particularly proud of your bio, share it with me—I'd love to hear from you! My contact details are included in the back of this book.

## Gratitude Is Everything

That's it! If you think about it, there's really just one step: Begin. Write your story. This all started with your passion. You've got this.

And remember, it's never going to be perfect. Nothing is ever perfect. Writing your bio will always be a work in progress.

I'd like to think that we humans are always striving to be better, to improve, to learn from our failures, to glean lessons from the success of others, to listen, and to be grateful. Part of writing a great bio is truly speaking to the needs of your audience, and that means showing gratitude for the people who need you most.

Speaking of gratitude, I'd like to close with a final story about rock stars. Years ago, before my life in publishing, back in the early '90s I was eyeliner deep in the music industry. Back then, record stores and radio DJs controlled what the public heard—they decided who got to be rock stars. Consequently, most of the rock stars I met were incredibly generous, but there were always those few who thought themselves better and were straight-up rude to their fan base. (I won't name names.) They had forgotten how they got their fame to begin with (from the loyalty of their fans). That kind of behavior always made me sad for them. They were missing out on so much and were likely stunting their own potential for success.

A few years back, my sister and I went to see Bruce Springsteen in Los Angeles. (It was awesome.)

I walked away humbled by his generosity. He gave a spectacular show, of course, but I'm a fan, so I would say that, right? But this was different. I had never witnessed a music icon give himself so completely to his fans. As he expressed his sincere love for his fans, the energy and gratitude became palpable. He sang as he walked along a catwalk that led him deeper into the heart of the audience, and I don't mean the kind of catwalk that elevated him far above the crowd—he was *in* the crowd. They had total access to him. At one point I was actually scared for his safety as a sea of hands engulfed him (and his guitar). But he leaned back into them, falling onto all those hands willingly. The crowd did their part by carrying him forward, back toward the stage, crowd-surfing style. Sure, I had seen this many times before, but there was something different and special about it this time. He wasn't drunk, or an egomaniac—he utterly gave himself to his audience. He expressed gratitude in a way that made me appreciate him even more.

It made me realize that without an audience, a rock star is just a human with a microphone. And, by the way, a superhero without a superpower is just a human in a silly get-up.

## Find Your Superpower

Be the best you can be. Write your bio with gratitude, and be great. And, always listen and strive to be even greater.

The world needs more greatness.

The world always needs more gratitude!

### Your Bio Checklist

★ Does your bio clearly state what you do?

★ Does your personality shine through?

★ Does it identify your credibility and tout your accomplishments?

★ Did you remember to include awards or contests you've won?

★ Did you include prominent associations or organizations you belong to in your industry?

★ Does it tell your readers why you are qualified to do what you do?

★ Does it tell your readers how you can help them?

★ Does it have a call to action that tells your readers what to do next?

★ Does it make you blush a little?

Good, you did it right.

Nothing is original. Steal from anywhere that resonates with inspiration or fuels your imagination.

—Jim Jarmusch, film director

# PART THREE

# REBECCA SWIFT

## Before

Rebecca Swift has a Masters in Education and taught in public schools for 12 years. As a teacher she had special training from the NOYCE Foundation and became a writing workshop demonstration teacher for her district. Since then she has written a soon-to–be-published memoir about finding her voice and her self-worth after years of living in the passenger seat of her own life. She is currently creating a couples relationship course with her therapist ex-husband that will be offered in the fall of 2018.

## Analysis

Rebecca sounds interesting. After all, she is working with her ex-husband. But, I'm not sure what is relevant about her teaching credentials; the benefits to me are not apparent. Also, I'm not sure why she's offering a relationship course. Technically we now know something about this author, but it fails to tell the reader what's in it for her. As a reader, what exactly do I get out of it?

This is a typical case of saying too little; we'll need to bulk this up a bit and make it about the reader, while also connecting the dots of Rebecca's "why": *Why* is she an expert? *Why* should I trust her? Plus, I want to add personality and ensure that Rebecca's superpower shines through.

## Using the Bio Formula

| | |
|---|---|
| **Goals** | Establish Rebecca as an author and thought leader on female empowerment, intimacy, and relationships<br><br>Sell her books<br><br>Build a loyal following of her writing and online workshops |
| **Superpower** | Empathy + Relator |
| **Audience** | Women who have dealt with self-worth issues and are looking (right now) for the courage to believe they are worthy and valuable and deserve it all; they are ready to believe it and put in the work<br><br>Educated<br><br>Ages 38 to 58 |
| **Influencers** | Esther Perel<br><br>Glennon Doyle Melton<br><br>Gracie X |

### Finding the Gold

In this situation, we don't have the benefit of the information dump that you will do to get it all down (Step 5), so we will have to pull from what we do have in her original bio. Let's identify the elements that stand out and then plug them into the formula.

I want to rethink the overall message and story of Rebecca. Below, I highlight everything that jumps out at me as possibly relevant.

Rebecca Swift has a Master's in Education and taught in public schools for 12 years. As a teacher she had special training from the NOYCE Foundation and became a writing workshop demonstration teacher for her district. Since then she has written a soon-to–be-published memoir about finding her voice and her self-worth after years of living in the passenger seat of her own life. She is currently creating a couples relationship course with her therapist ex-husband that will be offered in the fall of 2018.

## Applying the Bio Formula

Let's plug our ingredients into our formula.

1. **Focus**: What does she do exactly?
   Teacher, soon-to-be-published author of a memoir.

2. **Grabber**: Why do I care?
   She writes about finding her voice and her self-worth; she helps other women do the same.

3. **Credibility**: Why is she qualified to help me?
   Her experience gives her real life credibility; she found her voice, took back her power, and wrote a book about it!

4. **Promise**: What (specifically) does she offer me?
   A self-help book, couples relationship course *(empowerment)*.

5. **More**: What other credibility does she have?
   Teacher for 12 years, special training from the NOYCE Foundation.

6. **CTA (call-to-action)**: What does she want people to do?
   She's creating a relationship course for couples, eventually buy her book.

### What's Missing?

We have facts, yes, but nothing that speaks to me directly as reader. Nothing tells me how Rebecca can help me. Do we need t know that her business partner is her ex-husband? The first thing would ask Rebecca is why is she writing about relationships? Wh is she passionate and/or qualified to hold workshops? And how ca she help me? Don't you get the feeling that she's holding back o something? This is where the courage piece might come in—Rebecc needs to find the courage to shout her truth to the world. I ha the benefit of working with Rebecca, so I know what's missing, an you're about to find out in her Supercharged Bio, below.

Lastly, there is no call to action. If I read this bio, I might sa "Oh, that's nice," but there's nothing to engage me to stay connecte with Rebecca.

Below is a revised version that speaks to the reader about h needs, while also making Rebecca's story interesting and addin authority to her teaching credentials.

## Check Out Rebecca's Supercharged Bio

Rebecca Swift is an author, speaker, and advocate for self-awarenes and female empowerment. After years of living life in the passeng seat of her own life, Swift found the courage to believe in hersel find her voice, and claim her self-worth. Her forthcoming memoi *Example Title*, chronicles her journey from a once-stale monogamou marriage to a polyamorous one that not only saved her self-wort but it saved her marriage. Rebecca's intimate and honest account o her own personal transformation shows how believing you deserv more is sometimes the first step to healing.

Rebecca has a Master's in Education with special training fron the NOYCE Foundation to lead writing workshops; she is now usin her experience and passion to help mid-life women find and clair their own voice. She is also co-creating a relationship course that focuses on actionable tools for empowerment and healing.

For instant access to Rebecca's self-awareness and exploration journaling tools, to learn more about her relationship courses, and for early access to her forthcoming memoir, sign up at Example.com.

# MELISSA WRIGHT

## Before

Over twenty years' experience in higher education, human resources, and employment law.

Melissa received her Bachelor of Arts from the University of California at Los Angeles, with a major in political science and a minor in history.

She obtained her law degree from the San Francisco Law School.

While in law school, Melissa served as a founding member of the *International Law Journal.* She also completed a clerkship at the California Attorney General's Office, Criminal Division, and served as an Immigration Clinic volunteer. Melissa also received training and served as a volunteer mediator for the Small Claims Mediation Services at the Superior Court of California, County of San Diego.

Melissa became a member of the California bar in 2003.

Melissa began her career in higher education as a departmental human resources manager.

Melissa is an accomplished strategist, trusted advisor, and creative problem solver with strong analytical skills and political savvy. Her expertise in these areas have allowed her to successfully assist individuals as they identify the root causes of conflict, understand applicable laws and policies, determine risk tolerance and goals, and create and implement appropriate solutions.

Using these skills, Melissa has also successfully led numerous critical initiatives, including important gender-bias studies, from conception to completion.

Melissa is able to effectively communicate in writing and has extensive experience drafting and revising employment policies, providing issues summaries and position papers, developing informal resolution proposals, writing legal briefs, and formulating sensitive correspondence.

She is a formally trained mediator with a proven track record of successfully resolving complex disputes without litigation.

Melissa is a strong negotiator with extensive experience structuring and drafting contracts, settlement documents, performance management plans, collective bargaining agreements, and other correspondence.

Additionally, Melissa has significant experience conducting and supervising workplace investigations and administrative hearings and has also served as a hearing officer for student disciplinary cases.

She is also a skilled presenter and instructor and has developed training programs and given numerous talks on a variety of human resources topics.

Melissa has achieved outstanding results and is dedicated to helping all of her clients realize their goals.

## Analysis

Impressive. There is a lot here, but it reads like a laundry list and doesn't speak to me directly.

Melissa's goals are not solely based around getting new clients; she wants to land speaking engagements and get media interviews too. So this bio needs to humanize her and make her sound both impressive and approachable. Just a little of her CV will go along way in a shorter bio. Let's review her goals and take another shot at it.

## Using the Bio Formula

| | |
|---|---|
| **Goals** | Establish Melissa as an expert consultant in academic discrimination<br><br>Help women break through discrimination and build lasting, joyful careers without the need for litigation<br><br>Become a known testifier and media darling<br><br>Build her consulting business |
| **Superpower** | Command + Activator + Communicator |
| **Audience** | Women and minorities, ages 28–48, in academia who are struggling with discrimination and unsure how to navigate the waters without destroying their careers. |
| **Influencers** | Gloria Allred<br><br>Lisa Bloom<br><br>Caryn Groedel |

## Check Out Melissa's Supercharged Bio

Melissa Wright is a fierce lawyer, impassioned activist, and ardent advocate for those facing discrimination, harassment, retaliation, or other challenges in academia and the workplace. Through her lectures and appearances, she educates and empowers individuals to communicate effectively, make informed decisions confidently, and ultimately succeed in their respective fields.

With more than twenty years' experience in higher education, human resources, and employment law, Wright's unique perspective allows her to successfully assist individuals as they identify the root causes of conflict, understand applicable laws and policies, determine risk tolerance and goals, and create and implement appropriate solutions that avert or minimize harm and ultimately avoid litigation.

A member of the California Bar since 2003, Wright holds a BA in political science from UCLA and received a Juris Doctor from SFLS. At UCLA, she served as the Director of Academic Employee Relations, Senior Advisor and Director of Academic Policy Development, and served as the Assistant Vice Chancellor for Academic Personnel.

Wright is a formally trained mediator, a passionate presenter and instructor, and a highly sought-after speaker. She has represented and advised hundreds of individuals at universities and academic institutions, including UCLA, UCSD, Stanford, Johns Hopkins, NASA, Scripps Research Institute, the Smithsonian, Florida Institute of Technology, Cornell, Duke, and many more. To learn more about Mrs. Wright, hire her, or book her as a speaker, visit Example.com.

# STELLAR BIO EXAMPLES

 **Awesome Writing Coach + Thought Leader: Marni Freedman**

**Long Bio: 374 words**

Marni Freedman (BFA, LMFT) is a produced, published, and award-winning writer. After graduating as an award-winning student from the USC School of Filmic Writing, Marni began her career with *Two Goldsteins on Acid*, which was produced for the stage in Los Angeles. She worked as a script doctor for top film companies and worked as a script agent for the Mary Sue Seymour Agency. One of her plays was made into a film, *Playing Mona Lisa*, and was produced by Disney. Her award-winning play, *A Jewish Joke*, appeared Off Broadway in 2019. Her most recent play, *Roosevelt: Charge The Bear* debuted in New York in October of 2019.

Marni is the co-founder and Programming Director for The San Diego Writers Festival, runs the San Diego Writers Network, is the programming director for the San Diego Memoir Writers Association, and is editor of *Shaking the Tree: Brazen. Short. Memoir,* a yearly Anthology published by MCM Publishing.

Marni is also a therapist for artists and writers. Her welcoming, easygoing nature and solid background are the underpinnings of what makes her such a popular writing coach across the country. Marni is unique because she has a tool for almost everything; she has a way of taking complicated information and translating it into easy-to-grasp, step-by-step information. Her character worksheets and plotting devices have been met with rave reviews. She teaches writing workshops for UCSD Extension and at conferences and retreats across the country, and she runs the Memoir Certificate Program at San Diego Writers Ink.

Marni's most recent book, *Permission to Roar: For Female Thought Leaders Ready to Write,* won four awards and is an Amazon Bestseller. She also wrote *7 Essential Writing Tools: That Will Absolutely Make Your Writing Better (And Enliven the Soul)* and is currently writing her third book, *Write to Magic.*

She lives with her wonderfully talkative husband and son and their two cats, Dorothy J. Witten and The Beef, who don't like each other. Within her community she is often referred to as Glenda, the Good Witch of Writing. You can also find Marni at TheFeistyWriter.com, a writing hub to help writers find and believe in their authentic voice, and subscribe to her award-winning newsletter, filled with author tips and resources, at MarniFreedman.com.

## Short Bio: 143 words

Marni Freedman (BFA, LMFT) is a popular writing coach and award-winning author. She is co-founder of the San Diego Writers Festival and is a produced, published, and award-winning playwright. After graduating from the USC School of Filmic Writing, Marni began her career with her play, *Two Goldsteins on Acid,* which was produced in Los Angeles. She worked as a script doctor for top film companies and worked as a script agent. One of her plays, *Playing Mona Lisa,* was made into a film and was produced by Disney. She teaches at San Diego Writers Ink and UCSD Extension and produces a yearly theatrical Memoir Showcase. Most recently, Marni received multiple awards for both her touring one-man show, *A Jewish Joke,* and for her latest book, *Permission to Roar: For Female Thought Leaders Ready to Write Their Book.* Get writing tips and resources at marnifreedman.com.

## Fun, Hip Lawyer Guy: Sam Mazzeo

This one's super fun and totally not your typical bio, but I've included it because it shows that sometimes showing personality is more important than being pro, even for a lawyer.

### Casual Bio: 114 words

Sam realized pretty quickly that he was swimming upstream when it came to normal lawyering. Filing lawsuits? Arguing in court? Defending collections proceedings? No thanks! He currently spends his time sending GIFS to clients in between filing trademarks and drafting contracts. He has also served on some legit local boards like TEDxSanDiego and Think Dignity.

Sam has a lot of tattoos for being a lawyer. Just saying.

Interesting facts:

- He served as in-house legal counsel at Invisible Children
- He worked for Oceana, helping improve marine areas and improve salmon fisheries
- He learned to do a standing backflip for a Teen Wolf costume.

His bar number is 279934.

See all the serious stuff here: linkedin.com/in/sam-mazzeo.

★ **Bad Ass Book Mama and Author: Linda Silversten**

**Long Bio: 362 words**

Linda Silversten (aka "Book Mama") is a book proposal doctor, author whisperer, agent connector, idea fairy, and huge-hearted cheerleader of creativity for writers of all genres—and every gold-plated publishing dream. In the past 18 years, Linda has authored and co-authored nine books (two *New York Times* bestsellers), including the digital bestseller *Your Big Beautiful Book Plan* with Danielle LaPorte, *Generation Green* (Simon & Schuster), *Lives Charmed* (HCI), and *Harmonic Wealth* (Hyperion). She's the creator of *The Boyfriend Log* iPhone app (the first-ever app to track the health of any relationship/s... "because love can be confusing, and clarity is queen"); host of the top-rated literature podcast, *Beautiful Writers Podcast*–where she interviews many of the world's most beloved authors for candid behind-the-scenes conversations; and mama of the Beautiful Writers Group (a writerly membership community). Her recent TEDWomen talk on Time Debt has given language to something nearly everyone wrestles with but few have ever heard of.

Every few months Linda takes four or five women and a personal chef to Carmel-by-the-Sea, California, where she helps aspiring authors find their voice, birth their best books, and land agents and book deals at her intimate writing retreats overlooking the Pacific Ocean. *Carmel* magazine recommends these retreats in their profile, "The Word Wizard."

Linda and her work have been featured on *CNN*, *E!*, *Extra*, the *New York Times*, the *International Business Times*, *NY Post*, *Family Circle*, *Teen Vogue*, and the *Huffington Post*. She's written for all sorts of media, including the *Los Angeles Times* and *The Daily Love*, received wide coverage on her app, and been featured on *Inc.*, Forbes.com, Glamour.com, MarieClaire.com, and SheBrand's "You Should Know Her" column. Read about her podcast in the recent *The Motley Fool's* "10 Best Podcasts for Women," and find her blogging at BookMama.com (with a "Best of the Web" nod from *The Daily Muse*).

Having dreamed of being a writer as a child in Northern California, Linda's now living her dream, having helped countless talented clients polish their ideas, write proposals (with some fast and furious bidding wars in the 6—and even 7—figures!), and get their name and books out into the world where they belong.

## Short Bio: 199 words

Linda Sivertsen is a *New York Times* bestselling co-author and midwife of 6- and 7-figure book deals at her bimonthly writing retreats in Carmel-by-the-Sea, CA, recently profiled in *Carmel* magazine. She's the creator of *The Boyfriend Log* iPhone app ("because love can be confusing, and clarity is queen"), the host of the popular *Beautiful Writers Podcast* on iTunes, and co-creator of both Your Big Beautiful Book Plan and The Beautiful Writers Group. Her TEDWomen talk on Time Debt has given language to something nearly everyone wrestles with but few have ever heard of. Linda and her work have been featured on *CNN, E!, Extra*, the *New York Times*, the *NY Post*, *International Business Times, Family Circle, Teen Vogue*, and the *Huffington Post*. She's written for all sorts of media, including the *Los Angeles Times* and *The Daily Love*, received wide coverage on her app, and been featured on *Inc.*, Forbes.com, Glamour.com, MarieClaire.com, and SheBrand's "You Should Know Her" column. Read all about her podcast in the recent *The Motley Fool's* "10 Best Podcasts for Women," and find her blogging at BookMama.com (with a "Best of the Web" nod from *The Daily Muse*).

Find Linda on Facebook, Twitter, Instagram, and Pinterest.

## Facebook Goddess + Social Media Thought Leader: Mari Smith

**Website Bio: 490 words**

Mari Smith is the premier facebook marketing expert and social media thought leader.

Often referred to as "the Queen of Facebook," Mari Smith is one of the world's foremost experts on Facebook marketing. She is a Forbes' perennial Top Social Media Power Influencer, author of *The New Relationship Marketing* and coauthor of *Facebook Marketing: An Hour a Day.*

In 2015, Facebook headhunted Mari to partner with as the company's leading Small Business and Facebook Marketing expert, where she facilitated and taught at the Boost Your Business series of live training events across the United States.

IBM recently named Mari as one of seven women who are shaping digital marketing alongside Alex Hisaka, head of global content marketing at LinkedIn; Alison J Herzog, director global social business strategy at Dell; Susan Wojcicki, CEO of YouTube; and Adrienne Lofton, SVP of global brand marketing at Under Armour.

Fast Company described Mari as "A veritable engine of personal branding, a relationship marketing whiz and the Pied Piper of the Online World." Forbes named Mari as one of the Top Ten Social Media Power Influencers many years in a row, and Dun & Bradstreet Credibility named Mari one of the top ten Most Influential Small Business People on Twitter.

Mari's background includes almost two decades in the fields of online, offline, and relationship marketing, as well as internet technology. As a passionate social media leader since 2007, Mari travels the United States and internationally to provide engaging social media keynotes and in-depth training to entrepreneurs and corporations.

Mari often shares prestigious stages with notable leaders and celebrities; previous co-presenters have included Sir Richard Branson, the Dalai Lama, Eckhart Tolle, Tony Robbins, Paula Abdul, Chip Conley, and Arianna Huffington, to name a few.

Through her training services, Mari teaches businesses and brands to properly monetize their social media efforts, with measurable KPIs from integrating proven social media marketing strategies. After applying Mari's methods, her clients typically achieve significant increases in traffic, subscribers, lead generation and conversion, client growth, affiliates, lucrative strategic alliances, and targeted media attention.

Mari Smith and her team have mentored countless social media departments and individual social media professionals in a variety of specializations. Plus, tens of thousands of business owners and marketers from around the world have attended Mari's popular social media webinars over the past several years.

With her popular blog at MariSmith.com and her large, loyal following on Facebook, Twitter, Instagram, and LinkedIn, Mari is considered one of the top resources and thought leaders in the world of marketing. She regularly appears in media locally and nationally in publications such as the *New York Times*, the *Wall Street Journal, Inc., Forbes, Fortune*, the *Chicago Tribune*, and *Success* magazine.

On a personal note, Mari is Scottish-Canadian; she was born in Ontario, Canada, spent her childhood in a small rural Quaker community in BC, Canada, and then lived in Scotland for two decades before moving to San Diego, California, in 1999.

**Speaker Bio: 234 words**

Mari Smith is a renowned social media thought leader and one of the world's foremost experts on Facebook marketing. She is author of *The New Relationship Marketing* and coauthor of *Facebook Marketing: An Hour a Day*, both published by Wiley.

Facebook hired Mari to keynote, teach, and provide 1:1 consultations with attendees at the Boost Your Business U.S. tour in 2015.

Fast Company describes Mari as "A veritable engine of personal branding, a relationship marketing whiz and the Pied Piper of the Online World." Forbes named Mari one of the Top Ten Social Media Power Influencers four years in a row. Dun & Bradstreet Credibility named Mari one of the most influential small business people on Twitter.

Through her consulting and training business, Mari helps businesses to accelerate their profits by integrating proven social media marketing strategies. She also travels the United States and internationally to share her wisdom and provide social media keynotes and in-depth training. Plus, Mari mentors up-and-coming social media professionals in a variety of specializations.

With her popular blog and her large, loyal following on Facebook, Twitter, and Google+, Mari is considered one of the top resources and thought leaders in the world of marketing. She regularly appears in media locally and nationally in publications such as the *New York Times*, the *Wall Street Journal, Inc.*, *Forbes*, *Fortune*, and *Success* magazine.

Mari is Scottish-Canadian and resides in San Diego, California.

# ABOUT JENIFFER THOMPSON

**Now it's my turn. Here's a little bit about me.**

Jeniffer Thompson is a personal branding expert and digital marketing strategist. She is an award-winning publisher, author, and speaker who is passionate about delivering strategy-rich content and actionable tools that educate and empower authors and speakers. Since founding her company, Monkey C Media, in 2004, she and her team have been creating award-winning book cover designs and author websites that integrate digital marketing strategies that work!

With a BA in Journalism from SDSU, Jeniffer is an ardent believer in the power of storytelling—she is always looking for, or telling, a story. She believes that story has the power to heal, transform, and create community. She is a co-founder of the San Diego Writers Festival and serves on the board of the San Diego Memoir Writers Association. She is currently writing her own coming-of-age memoir entitled *The Paper Tiger*.

Jeniffer is a rock climber and thrill seeker. She lives in San Diego with her husband, Chad, their persnickety Manx cat, Mishka, and three fluffy chickens who love to follow her around and give her delicious eggs (almost) everyday.

For awesome brand strategy tips and digital marketing insight, subscribe to her blog and download her 10 Steps to Personal Branding at JenifferThompson.com.

## And a little bit more, just for you, oh, beautiful reader:

Follow me on any one, or all, of these social hot spots:

| | |
|---|---|
| LinkedIn | linkedin.com/in/jenifferthompson |
| Facebook | facebook.com/jenifferthompsonconsulting |
| Twitter | twitter.com/jeniffergrace |
| Instagram | instagram.com/jeniffer_grace |

Plus, I have more books coming out this year and I'd love to get you on my list as an advance reader. Go to JenifferThompson.com for all the delicious details.

1. *Website Wow: Turn Your Website into Your Most Powerful Marketing Tool* (2nd Edition)

2. *Find Your Superpower: Personal Branding for Authors, Speakers, and Entrepreneurs*

3. *Hustle: Digital Marketing Strategies for Authors, Speakers, and Entrepreneurs*

4. *Smart Author Branding: How to Build a Loyal Tribe of Readers*

## Leave a Review!

If you found this book helpful, leave a review on Amazon and Goodreads. I'd be so grateful—it all helps!

# LINKS AND RESOURCES

I've developed a bevy of Smart Author Branding worksheets to help you on your journey, and added a few other resources for good measure. Check 'em out at **JenifferThompson.com/book-resources**.

- ★ Bio Profiles spreadsheet

- ★ Reader Persona worksheet

- ★ Brand Audit worksheet

- ★ Ten Things You Can Do Right Now
  to Kickstart Your Brand

- ★ Sources for Rights-Free Images
  (to make your social posts and blogs stand out)

- ★ Getting Organized Tips sheet

- ★ Smart Author Bio worksheet

- ★ Smart Author Bio Versions worksheet

- ★ *Permission to Roar: For Female Thought Leaders
  Ready to Write Their Book*

- ★ *Your Big Beautiful Book Plan*
  (how to write book proposals)

- ★ *7 Essential Writing Tools: That Will Absolutely Make Your
  Writing Better (And Enliven Your Soul)*

- ★ *The Chicago Manual of Style* (hardcover)

- ★ *Strengths Finder 2.0*

CPSIA information can be obtained
at www.ICGtesting.com
Printed in the USA
FSHW011647251019
63387FS